Finding Your Soft Cry

By Robert Villegas

Finding Your Soft Cry

By Robert Villegas

ISBN: 9798474165721

Imprint: Independently published

Robertv1989@outlook.com

www.robertvillegas.com

Made in the United States of America

Social Media Addresses

Parler: @Robertv1989

CloutHub @RobertVillegas

WimKin Robert Villegas

MeWe Robert Villegas

Minds @Robertv1989

Gab @V4Vendata

Photo by Johnny Cohen on Unsplash

Table of Contents

Every individual has a yearning to know that he is both free and good. This yearning comes to him from early youth, and he hopes to eventually develop the intellectual tools to distinguish between his nature and the demands of society. The key to freedom is the ability to act without restriction and, especially, without guilt.

You stand on your own in this moment of truth. The wonder you experience about life comes only when fear is gone, tension is gone, pain is gone and you are in your place of safety, looking both out and in, standing in the sunshine of your place of peace. Full acceptance of yourself is acceptance of existence and of happiness now and in the future. You've chosen the best ideas you could find; ideas that bring you success and fulfillment You enjoy understanding them and have made them part of every day and part of every thought. You to face life with confidence and complete self-assurance. Your future is now; made up of your best thoughts and a commitment to total mastery overall. This is how you are supposed to feel when you know you are good and free. "It is what you know that has made you the person you are."[1]

---

[1] Rational Meditation by Robert Villegas https://amzn.to/2PWMCAy (Paid Link)

But what happens when you are confronted with the demands of people who have no good intentions? What if those intentions conflict with your principles and your peace of mind? It is at this point when you cry a soft cry, when you realize you are suffering the realization of your position as a subject and not as a free individual.

"All of you here … are suffering. And, indirectly or directly, are counting on capitalism as the only hope of relief. You are suffering in one form or another from Washington, from government strangulation of the economy, from a torrent of government caused evils which keep getting worse year after year, such as an ominous inflation and now the signs of a recession, and an energy crisis and burgeoning taxation and burgeoning bureaucrats stifling business, and burgeoning … pressure groups demanding still more regulation. In other words, from controls which are now out of control."[2]

This book will examine the danger and suffering that every individual suffers under the control of society, culture, and law. Feeling safe, being safe and feeling that one's love of life, are all chiseled away through small slights, small thefts, and small laws that add up to your soft cry.

---

[2] The Philosophic Basis of Capitalism by Leonard Peikoff Lecture Ayn Rand Institute

Many of us experience a lingering soft cry when we encounter various aspects of culture and society. I consider this soft cry to be part of an individual's sense of life, but it is also a psychological issue. To understand it, I'll explain how I think it begins.

As a young child many of us experience anger and abuse at the hands of older children or adults. Needless to say, we know that these incidents of abuse are imposed upon young people who have done nothing wrong. In some cases, it is called child abuse and in other cases it is called social leveling, a call for the individual to be shamed according to a dominant ethical norm. To begin, we'll do a short sweep over some common types of abuse.

The basis of the soft cry is the discomfort felt by the individual over treatment by others. This includes the discomfort felt by being treated unfairly, being falsely accused, being gaslighted, being hated, and not knowing the source of the hate.

The most primitive form of the soft cry is when there is no ulterior motive or ideology behind the abuser – just pure hate. The abuser could be someone once troubled in his or her life, and who chose the path of a teacher or religious leader. Or someone who has been the victim of similar treatment, once vulnerable or innocent who felt a subconscious need for revenge.

The most likely abuser is the individual who starts life with a sense of inferiority compared to other people. Because he does not understand why he feels this way, he tends to fake his feelings without knowing it. This faking is a faux acceptance, a sublimation of the soft cry that becomes chronic fear and hatred of others.

This abuser then begins a process of learning how to lie. He learns to manipulate the minds of other through pragmatism, gaslighting, professions of love and critical theory that "pretend" a feigned "love" and "regard" for those he seeks to manipulate and destroy.

The soft cry comes when the "abuse" is ideological, philosophical, critical (as in critical theory) and implicit. The soft cry is often attended by protestations of love and of the need to be loving to hide the implicit criticism and advance toward the cruelty of dictatorship.

Let us look at some examples of the soft cry. Philosopher Immanuel Kant declared, in his metaphysical writings, that the noumenal realm of existence is independent of perception (which means it can't be adequately perceived by the senses), while the phenomenal realm represents the world as it is, but man cannot fully comprehend it because the senses are vague and indeterminate.

The upshot of this view is that we can perceive neither the phenomenal realm nor the noumenal realm. One is vague and the other is blocked from consciousness. Why Kant decided that this would help understanding is a mystery to many, because, subconsciously, by this view, understanding is impossible – this makes Kant's view an attack on the individual's ability to understand and this creates a "soft cry" because the individual concludes he is weak intellectually and cognitively. Teachers influenced by Kant teach man that he must understand that he can't understand.

The practical lesson from this Kantian perspective leads the student down a cognitive dead end and the consequence subconsciously is what I call the "soft cry" – the feeling that the human mind is incapable of understanding. Man feels this attack on his mind, and it gives him a soft fear that leads to paranoia and schizophrenia. Kant is the deadliest killer of men because he has given them an understanding that they can't understand. The result is lack of confidence and disconnected knowledge.

Once the soft cry starts, the individual experiences subconscious paralysis which is the restriction of freely chosen action. In short, he does not know why he can't act for his own self-interest. Kant's attack on his mind is hidden under the pretense of teaching him something good. He does not realize that Kant's imposition of inefficacy has incapacitated him.

The soft cry creates paralysis until the individual is free of the subconscious thought left in him – free of the consequences of abuse. Just like any form of crying leads to temporary paralysis, until the individual is free of the soft cry, the individual will never be free. Because these premises are wordless, brought on by the hidden Kantian critique of human incompetence.

The hard cry, on the other hand, is much more intense because it involves threat of violence, actual violence, and a major loss of tangible values. The individual is left prostrate and often more conscious of the loss, whereas with the soft cry, the loss is implicit.

The soft cry has essentially the same impact on the mind and emotions (as does the hard cry), but it is hidden beneath the implicit premises of the Kantian critique and its derivative anti-concepts. The soft cry involves wordless thoughts and feelings which are more sinister and harmful, while the hard cry is animated by a more direct response (fight/flight/freeze) that is built into the human body as a response to fear, anxiety, and attack. The soft cry paralyzes wordlessly and is therefore longer lasting and has a more deadly impact on the mind.

In the chapter entitled "The Solution", I explain that there is a lost concept that provides the key to dealing with the problems created by the various attacks on the individual engaged by religion and modern philosophy.

The Soft Cry of Gaslighting

Gaslighting causes the soft cry because it challenges the individual's view of reality, and this causes insecurity. When an individual is gaslighted, it leaves him wondering what is wrong with him.

In my book, "The Call to Reason", I wrote about gaslighting:

"Gas lighting is "… a form of psychological abuse where a person or group makes someone question their sanity, perception of reality, or memories. People experiencing gaslighting often feel confused, anxious, and unable to trust themselves."[3]

The quoted article also gives us a list of common gaslighting techniques"

- Countering the words of the victim.
- Withholding information from the victim.
- Trivializing the ideas of the victim.
- Denial of the perceptions of the victim.
- Diverting the victim to other issues.
- Stereotyping and name calling of the victim.

Another form of gaslighting (that I have discovered) is the practice of hiding the truth through careful information leaking. A good (or should I say terrible) way of gaslighting is done through the organization

---

[3] https://www.medicalnewstoday.com/articles/gaslighting

of "events", "knowledge" and "conclusions" to lead people to conclusions about actual events that do not conform with the truth. For example, hiding the truth was done during the events of America's surrender in Afghanistan during the summer of 2021. The truth is that President Biden made some obvious strategic mistakes that caused the deaths of many people. To hide the truth that Biden was in the process of hiding the truth of decisions and events, a careful effort was engaged to reorganize events in ways that left him and his administration blameless for his boneheaded decisions.

Another form of gaslighting is the practice of hiding the truth about the value of capitalism. This was accomplished by the same intellectuals who brought us critical theory. What many people don't realize is that critical theory is fundamentally "critical" of capitalism. They created, in a sense, a "science of society" or sociology that "proved" that capitalism was racist, exploitative, murderous, harmful to society and values. Critical theory was essentially pseudo-science that sought to advance socialism and destroy the only system that brought prosperity and affluence. Because critical theorists pretended to be scientific, they were largely successful in destroying capitalism, even though many critical theory scholars had escaped the dictatorship of the Nazis by coming to America and using their critical theories to denigrate capitalism.

Critical theorists such as Herbert Marcuse taught students who later transformed critical theory into critical race theory. Both concepts are efforts to gaslight people. In fact, CRT is not only about race; it is also an attack against capitalism. By accusing certain "races" of endemic racism, critical race theorists connect "white people" to capitalism which adds strength to the arguments of critical theorists. Critical race theory is, then, not only racism, but a brutal form of gaslighting against all (so-called) races.

Any gaslighted individual, to the extent that he or she is manipulated by this method, becomes severely clouded intellectually and his self-confidence is diminished. The impact on the ego (since he has no choice about being a racist) destroys his ability to understand concepts and their meanings. The result of these impacts is the soft cry and a vulnerable individual

The Soft Cry of Philosophical Gaslighting

I discussed philosophical gaslighting in the first chapter of this book. In my book "The Call to Reason", I also wrote about it:

"The evilest form of gaslighting is what I call "philosophical gaslighting" which was engaged by philosophers to destroy the student's ability to ascertain reality. Both metaphysical gaslighting and epistemological gaslighting are used by philosophers such as Kant, Hume, and the pragmatists to declare that reality exists but man cannot see it, or that reality does not exist so man can never understand it.

""Man is, therefore, a creature in metaphysical conflict, a dual creature—much more deeply so than the enlightenment (or even the medieval era) imagined; he is, so to speak, a metaphysical biped, with one (unreal) foot in the phenomenal world, and one (unknowable) foot in the noumenal world."[4]

""Kant is the cruel destroyer of the mind who makes slaves of all mankind through the intellectual vacuum he has created in the mind. There can be no knowledge if there is no reality. Man can only experience incompetence and conflict with the world. This is the world that modern philosophy (as

---

[4] Kant and Self-Sacrifice by Leonard Peikoff, The Objectivist Newsletter—September 1971

the intellectual Master) creates for men so they have no hope of certainty."[5]

Who is the philosophically gaslighted individual? Essentially, the victim is any person influenced by Humean/Kantian philosophies (almost everybody). This includes progressives, pragmatists, mystics, and others who attempt to practice the Kantian view of the nature of reality and man's relation with it.

What is the mechanism that creates the harm of philosophical gaslighting? There are essentially three influences from these philosophers. The first is conceptual (or epistemological). The second is metaphysical (the nature of reality) and the third is a combination of collectivism and altruism.

This last is the consequence of the other two. What is man to do with his life if he cannot understand the phenomenal realm nor experience the noumenal realm? The only thing he can do, Kant would tell him, is create reality out of the categories of his mind and this leads him to the imperative to duty and self-sacrifice.

At this point, the soft cry of anti-conceptuality arrives to control his life, making him easy pickings for the Church and the government.

---

[5] The Call to Reason by Robert Villegas

Pseudo-Science is false science. It masquerades as real science, but it is essential a vehicle for jumping to conclusions to support a false proposition.

In my book, "The Call to Reason", I wrote:

"Practicing science is a demanding project. It requires integrity and a respect for the truth. But it is also a highly technical field that requires conceptual clarity, precise definitions, and testable observations. In short, it signals the importance of the individual and his independent mind. This means that for the independent individual, the mind is central to living well and science is a tool of the mind.

One thing a true scientist never does is draw a conclusion and then look for the facts to support it. That is not science. In fact, petitio principii is "a logical fallacy in which a premise is assumed to be true without warrant or in which what is to be proved is implicitly taken for granted."[6]

In fact, one cannot do science if one engages in any of the several informal logical fallacies. You can find lists of them on several Internet sites. And there is a reason why they are called fallacies: they do not work in the real world. Science is about the evidence of the senses and utilizing observation and testing of

---

[6] https://www.merriam-webster.com/dictionary/petitio%20principii

reality so we can drill down into the foundation of knowledge and then move up from there to more advanced and abstract propositions.

Yet, as we have seen, there are very few people offering science to Americans and many people offering pseudo-science in the name of science. How is this situation to be reconciled? How can we change the culture and start using real science?

So how can I prove I am right? The only way is to show you that most of the things you have come to believe are wrong and the preponderance of the evidence is that you are being fed pseudo-scientific lies The practice of using pseudo-science to prove an important point has been exposed by a group of college professors who have pointed the finger at their colleagues in the universities and shown how they are fostering pseudo-science for political purposes – which makes this form of lie critically important.

Here is the tactic for practicing pseudo-science:

1. Identify a Marxist idea that you want the bulk of society to accept.
2. Have a group of professors do a study about a faux problem you would like to "fix".
3. Then have other professors write what are called "peer reviewed articles" about the study and mostly agree that the study is valid.

4. Then expand the original idea by having other professors do more studies that expand the broad reach of the original study.

5. Then have other professors write books about the original idea and how it works in society, how it has worked in history (all of which are over-generalizations), how it is validated by "science", how people should change their minds and adopt political programs and regulations which assume the veracity of the original idea.

6. Now, students in the universities will be required to read these books, write reports on them, get graded on their reports and take their "learning" home to their communities and corporations to transform society and encourage people to think the way the professors want.

7. All of this for an unproven idea.

Now, I want to remind you that the original proposition that started this steamroller was a lie. Yet, Marxists insist that their ideas are new and unique. They have no problem recycling old Marxist ideas because they think you have forgotten history. Once again, the lie is the truth and people can be punished or ostracised if they do not agree with the lie. Ad nauseum."

Another form of pseudo-science is called "idea laundering". Idea laundering is not as complicated as some think. It is essentially the practice of advancing a pseudo-scientific proposition such as "all whites are racist" and then manipulating history and historical facts into an idea that is supposedly true. Once accepted as true, the college professors begin teaching students that the idea is true beyond a doubt and then grading students on that basis. As more "peer reviewed" studies and essays are published, students are led to think there is no doubt about the "fact" that all whites are racists. Eventually, these students go into the "real world". They become teachers, college professors, business leaders, politicians and CEOs and they bring this premise with them to inform their teachings, practices, and decisions. In this way, the entire society becomes informed by the laundered idea and society suffers from the false notion. If you disagree, you are a racist and people should not deal with you. If you agree, you are cognitively impaired and you don't know why your institutions, corporations and careers are failing.

As the universities plunge deeper into idea laundering, usable knowledge will be lost, and the university mind will become further enmeshed in ideas that do not correspond to the real world. Truth and the past will be forever lost until someone discovers that the ideas being used by people are causing individual and social failure everywhere. As collectivism and the sacrifice preached by altruism become even stronger, there will be a gradual decline in knowledge and the quality of research suffers. The individual will lose his autonomy, his free mind, and the ability to disagree with others. The soft cry of being an outsider will destroy many people, suicide rates will increase, and few people will know that the orgy of collectivism and sacrifice mean the destruction of joy, freedom, and innovation.

The next form that induces the soft cry is what I call value destruction or the triumph of the zero, otherwise known as altruism. Altruism is a demand of the soul. The moral code advocated by altruist states (fascist, communist, and socialist) demand that man give up his values for others. It holds that others are superior to the individual and that it is his duty to live for others.

When you use your intelligence and energy to produce value to trade with others, altruism holds that you are doing something evil, and you owe that production to others. It also holds that when society allows you to keep a small portion of your production, it is allowing you to do something evil. In fact, some of the worst atrocities today are done in the name of altruism. Virtually every major catastrophe in the world today is caused by or exacerbated by the demand for altruist sacrifice. Examples of altruism's evil include the following:

- China demands that its citizens sacrifice for the state (from each according to his ability to each according to his needs). This is the invocation of individual sacrifice under the premise that sacrifice will help society. This is "the greatest good" argument that requires the individual give up his values for others.

This also happened in the Soviet Union and other countries that went over to communism or socialism. The soft cry here has had devastating effects on human history and caused many deaths (Remember the Red Purge). People still haven't realized how evil this idea is.

- The various wars that the United States has been involved with are altruistic wars; sacrifice of our soldiers and military to "save" others and their nations from their own governments. The result is the loss of numerous American lives as sacrificial victims.
- The re-distribution of income from productive Americans to non-productive is altruism. This is the theft of values and property and represents the "greater good" argument. A good example is the massive amounts of money taken by government that forces Americans to sacrifice (wrongly) for "the greater good".
- In schools, all children are trained on how to live for others. This puts tremendous social pressure on the child and makes him and her question their own value.

The social pressure of altruism is massive; it causes many children to question who they are as individuals. I submit they don't deserve the cruelty of being told to live for others. It sets them on a negative path and can cause serious damage throughout their entire lives.

The idea that you can only be moral if you live for others is destructive of your value and the values you create through thinking and production. It is even destructive of your future and your plans for a good life. It is the moral code of altruism that is responsible for this and the feeling it engenders in you can only be a soft cry about the unfairness of society.

In my book, The Logical Fallacy of Altruism, I used text from Ayn Rand's book Atlas Shrugged in which she wrote about "The Plan" that was an effort to insinuate altruism and collectivism into the operating rules of a large company called the Twentieth Century Motor Company. In one part of the chapter, she talks about the psychological consequences of total altruism. I would recommend that you read Atlas Shrugged to learn more about how altruism destroys societies and how the demand for sacrifice destroys lives and cooperation among men.[7]

---

[7] Atlas Shrugged by Ayn Rand

I also wrote about Re-distribution in this book:

"I have written extensively about the immorality of socialist re-distribution. To be specific, I recently wrote this:

"The thing about socialism; what people don't get about it (that makes it wrong) is its basic premise. I do not know why so many people do not see it. Marx said it explicitly: from each according to his ability to each according to his needs. Why do so many people think this is a noble idea? It is the most reprehensible idea of all.

"The "from" part is the first problem. When you take from someone you are taking his values that he worked for. That is not an act of kindness, it is an act of theft, and you can bet the person from whom things are taken does not like it. The "to" part is equally problematic. It tells the person receiving the other person's value that he does not have to earn his keep. All he needs to do is wait on the sidelines and someone else will take care of him. That attitude hardly breeds economic competence and a flourishing life. It breeds failure and incompetence.

"Any person with common sense will tell you that the so-called end of socialism can't happen. You can never take enough from the giver to take care of the receiver. It just isn't possible to provide all the food and affluence the receiver needs because that would mean total sacrifice from the giver, and beyond this, it would require the giver to produce twice as much (or more) for his own survival. That's why socialism always fails. It is an impractical idea. Noble? Hardly - corrupt is what it is. A false promise that fraudulently takes from the giver to cheat the receiver.

"Yet, socialists and BLM claim their idea of mass re-distribution of the social product is some sort of grand new scheme. When people remind them that this scheme must always fail, they declare that it is a good idea but that most men are not good enough to make it work. They proclaim that if only men would sacrifice for others instead of being selfish, then socialism would work.

"This is where we must remind ourselves of the notion that this very statement about men being "too selfish" is the justification for forcing men to sacrifice against their wills. Beyond this, it will become the justification for killing those who don't sacrifice which is what almost every socialist scheme of the past has done. What they ignore is that it is "just", for a person whose goods are being stolen, to reduce his effort so that more is not taken from him in the future. This is a fact of nature – you can't take life from life and expect life to continue.

"In order to erase the history of the genocides of the past, BLM must erase the memory of socialism, and they must declare that the idea is good, but men just aren't good enough for it. I submit that it isn't the productive people who are not good enough for socialism; these people are just fine, and they are the moral ones because they work hard to survive. The real people who cannot make socialism work are the misguided socialists and the "needy" people who don't want to carry their own weight. These people are not good for any society, capitalist, communist, fascist, or socialist. They just aren't good people. They are takers and not makers. There are thieves and not producers. And it is the takers who will destroy the "dream" of BLM and progressives for a utopian future. As always happens with utopian dreams, they become murderous nightmares.

"And these bad people are the people who are advocating Marxism in the BLM and other far left parties and organizations. The key to understanding Marxism is to see that it represents a philosophical movement derived from historical determinism, the idea that history is a movement of principles in conflict. To say that history is about capitalism versus socialism is likewise false knowledge, pseudo-science, and idea laundering.

"Socialism is always a false quest based in near religious mysticism, the projection of a rationalist dream made possible by mere words disconnected from reality. The unreality of historical materialism is what destroys people's lives, and societies. This is the result that BLM will accomplish.

"Today, the principle of historical determinism has been diluted and lost much of its meaning despite the fact that it is still the foundation of Marxism. Some Marxist groups still foster a sort of class struggle, but they place the struggle clearly upon the issue of race, converting the bourgeois class into "racist white supremacists" and placing Blacks into the "working class" seeking economic equality. Both of these premises are lies.

"Our society was not built by white supremacists. On the contrary, it is white people who have been at the forefront of the destruction of slavery as an institution in America. It is white people who have fought for individual suffrage in society and they have been at the forefront of building a capitalist society that offers every man of every color an opportunity to become an affluent "worker". It is capitalism, not socialism, that has liberated man throughout history. It is honest individuals who have fought for individual rights and capitalism. The Marxist critique of capitalism is the biggest lie of all, the biggest example of pseudo-science and idea laundering.

"Here is why capitalism is great:

1. It leaves you free to make all your own economic decisions. This includes the right of association, trade, property, and speech.

2. It leaves you free to work for an employer of your choice or to start your own company. The right of association.

3. It protects your money from confiscation by government. Individual rights and property rights.

4. It protects your property from confiscation by government. Property rights.

5. It does not demand that you sacrifice your time, energy, or money for the sake of people you do not know. Self-sufficiency, pride, and egoism.

6. It operates on the law of supply and demand which means your prices are determined by your decisions on what you buy. Freedom of trade and ownership.

7. It rewards you for hard work and good attitude. Virtue and virtuous living.

8. It rewards you regardless of your color. Color-blindness – this is an aspect of freedom and the right of association.

9. True capitalism does not allow for any kind of government regulation of business. Free market economics and/or capitalist freedom.

10. It is fully consistent with the constitution and with the principle of individual rights - this means you have rights, and the government cannot violate those rights.

11. It leaves you free to make your own mistakes, to learn from those mistakes and correct your harmful actions - in contrast to a socialist government that pays you not to work, that gives you money when you make the wrong decisions and that punishes producers to pay for your mistakes.

12. A capitalist society does not succumb to pseudo-science because bad ideas do not work in a society that fosters knowledge and science. Pseudo-science is the acceptance of a pre-determined conclusion and then seeking out "facts" to "prove" the conclusion. That's not how knowledge is developed – that's only how socialism and idea laundering are advanced. Freedom of ideas and thought.

13. Capitalism protects capital and the free use of capital. People are not taxed out of their capital, and

this frees capital to its best uses. If a capitalist sees his enterprise failing, he has the freedom to recoup his capital and invest it in job-producing activities. He is not forced to use his capital the way a government would dictate.

14. Capitalism protects the right of the seller to set the price he wants and the right of the buyer to buy at the price he wants. Law of supply and demand.

15. Capitalism recognizes that production must come before consumption. One cannot give people money to consume. Government must leave people free to produce and the market will decide winners and loser."[8]

Socialism is a scourge on society because of the demand that some men sacrifice their values for others and the inability of collectivism to organize society for the betterment of all. In fact, all the benefits of capitalism listed above are not available under socialism.

Socialism uses moral force to put a burden on every individual to accept the false notion that sacrificing is good for people, and that it does no harm to the productive individual. Socialism is the enemy of the producer because it impoverishes him and sends his money to be wasted, not on investment, but on

---

[8] Ibid

consumption. This loss of value (for the productive) harms society in general because it destroys production and impoverishes the producer by taking away from him the money he would otherwise use to invest in production.

Many of us do not feel the "scourge" of socialism because we are taught not to look at the amount of money taken from our paychecks each week. Yet, subconsciously, and daily, we must lower our heads a little more each day, so we don't see the gradual decline in our lives. Today, in the age of coronavirus, the decline becomes more evident every day. Yet, most people don't see that what is making their lives worse is the government's ability to dictate our actions, eliminate our pleasures and keep us, largely, away from other people. This is not about saving lives. It is about socialism and its hold on our society. Most seldom feel the soft cry in their lives, the soft loss of their souls, because they have been taught by the philosophy of altruism to feel good when they have been stolen from.

The Soft Cry and Egalitarianism

Another example that leads to a soft cry is the concept of egalitarianism. The idea that all men are metaphysically equal is the foundation of this idea. Egalitarianism means that differences among men do not count, and society should parcel out (re-distribute) benefits to individuals equally without regard to the individual's productive ability.

The question is: how did we decide that men were equal metaphysically when there is clear evidence that they are not equal by any means? Men are distinctly different in terms of the amount of effort they make, the intelligence they exert, the educational levels they pursue, and choices they make about their productive activities. I suggest that this "metaphysical" difference can only take place by denuding the term "metaphysics" of all meaning. Once the term is meaningless, then all differences in men's actions are meaningless as well.

But you can not arbitrarily change definitions of reality-based concepts and expect reality to comply. Word games have no positive impact on reality. They are caused by philosophical nominalism, the idea that definitions are loose approximations, and this leads to anti-concepts and confusion.

Egalitarianism is a call for the metaphysical equality of all men. An online dictionary defines it this way:

"Egalitarianism[9]

- *n.*

The political doctrine that holds that all people in a society should have equal rights from birth.

- *n.*

the doctrine of the equality of mankind and the desirability of political and economic and social equality."

In fact, I agree with this definition of egalitarianism. Yet, there is more to it than that. There is the issue of what you think man should do in society if you want to establish egalitarian objectives. For instance, the Founders declared "All men are created equal." But, by this they meant men are equal under the law, that no man should have a legal advantage over other men.

By contrast, modern egalitarianism (based on Marxist critical theory) has expropriated the term "equal" and changed it from "equality before the law" to "equality of results", ignoring the fact that to have equality of results, some men must be forced against their will to work for, or sacrifice for, that that idea.

____

[9] https://www.wordnik.com/words/egalitarianism

And, even beyond this, modern Marxists have appropriated a new term to seal the deal. Now, they are saying they want "equity".

What does "equity" mean?

You can only get terms like this from the gyrations made by the scholars of critical race theory (and idea laundering) which is an effort to use race to destroy capitalism by enslaving some "races".

In financial and property matters, the term "equity" means surplus assets or property. You define your equity by subtracting what you owe from the total value of your assets. All equity is expressed in terms of dollars. When I do a review of my financial condition, I express my surplus value (equity) in terms of dollars.

So, what do the Democrats in power mean when they say they are going to prioritize certain groups for equity. It can only mean government re-distribution of income from producers to special groups. Of course, this is tribalism, racism, discrimination, and collectivism.

"One of the reasons I'm so optimistic about this nation is that today's generation of young Americans is the most progressive, thoughtful, inclusive generation that America has ever seen. And they are pulling us toward justice in so many ways, forcing us to confront the huge gap in economic inequity, between those at the top and everyone else, forcing us to confront the existential crisis of climate. And yes, forcing us to confront systemic racism and white supremacy."[10]

If you don't feel a tinge of fear and a soft cry while listening to this, you are not a human being. What President Biden means here is that the Teachers Unions have been educating our students in progressive ideas. These include critical race theory, environmentalism, medical care as a right, radical leftist politics, revolution, re-distribution of income and many other exploitative concepts. He sees today's young adults as a valuable weapon because they will support his pragmatism and political agenda and, on top of this, money laundering, political voter fraud and massive spending all for the sake of forcibly taking money from some people (the productive) for the sake of the unproductive parasites who benefit from government.

To call this a free society is an insult to free societies.

It should not be hard to imagine how the idea of equity creates the soft cry. Imagine being told that you are required to give up your equality to others by means of the politically false idea of "equity", or

---

[10] Joe Biden Speech on Executive Orders for Racial Equity Transcript January 26 - Rev

being told that others have a claim on your income and savings because they have been deemed victims of *your* best effort. Such a false charge can only have a negative effect on your mind.

What you deserve is joy and freedom and the feeling of having the world open to you and your actions. Anything you produce is yours and no one should demand it from you. This applies to you if you are an average person, and it applies to billionaires such as Bill Gates and others.

Conservatives have often complained that major media companies are biased against them. We are going to ask the question "Why does the supposed unbiased media not report the right fairly? I'd like to approach this matter from a different perspective and that is from the left.

What does the left have against the right? Why is the media so dismissive of right-wing politicians, policies, and proposals? I'd like to suggest that the left thinks it is superior to the right intellectually and morally. It sees itself as born out of empiricism and skepticism. As empiricists, leftist think they are reality-based and thus more focused on the real while the right is more focused on God and mysticism. Therefore, the media feels justified in ignoring the right and refusing to cover them.

I would like to suggest that both the left and the right are wrong. They are both intellectually incompetent. Even though empiricism is a characteristic of the left, rationalism is based on floating characterizes, this makes them both cognitively incompetent. Rationalism is based on floating abstractions disconnected from reality. Empiricism is based upon anti-concepts disconnected from reality. Both views lead to cognitive failure and this leaves both incapable of leading mankind. I have written about how this is true under other cover, but I think the clear fact is that empiricism leads to concrete-bound thinking and rationalism leads to spiritism and floating abstractions. Both disconnect man's mind from reality.

I submit that the worst murder is to use ideas as weapons against the mind, and this is done by the media under the influence of both empiricism and rationalism. For the most part, our media was born of modern philosophy (empiricism) and its mother has bequeathed to it the ideas of Kant, Hume, Marx, and Dewey which have been mixed into an anti-conceptual soup called critical theory (the assumption that capitalism, individualism, and self-interest are evil). This soup is spiced by compromise, subterfuge and lies. History has shown that this mix does not end well.

If the ruling agenda is to promote a certain falsehood (anti-capitalism), then today's media considers it their duty "for the cause" to create content that "sells" people on the validity of the anti-capitalist agenda. So-called capitalists, schooled in pragmatism, violate the principles of logical thinking by falsely proclaiming logic and science, feeding men indeterminacy, anti-conceptualism, compromise, trial and error and bold leaps without principles. This can never work but it does indicate that gaslighting, lies and critical (anti-capitalist) theories are all they have. This makes it impossible for them to be understood and it exposes their inability to lead and help Americans prosper. Prosperity is not their goal – plunder and destruction are what they want.

Pragmatism in the universities teaches students how to think in reverse. They conclude that something is true if it works, meaning it is true if people believe it – the reverse is correct; a fact is true if it corresponds to reality, not because of the "beliefs" of others carefully insinuated into their minds. Because pragmatism cannot come up with solid facts, absolute truths, the efforts of pragmatists to "solve" problems through trial-and-error result in the lie that "we are making progress" (without a definition of what progress means) (Note the many protestations of progress made by military leaders during the 20-year war in Afghanistan that ended up in a massive disaster).

The truth is that people don't create reality by having the media tell them everything is progressing well under leftist policies. The role of consciousness is to find the truth and then accept it on that basis. Engineering their minds by carefully feeding today's talking points or this year's fantasy will not do it. The media thinks it is their job to convince you of their agenda and your acceptance of it would mean that it is a true agenda. There is no truth there. People's minds do not create reality; their only ability is to ascertain it. Lies can do nothing to influence reality because they are the opposite of reality; hence, reverse think in virtually every way. This is all the left can do – lie.

As I wrote above, the agenda for the pragmatist media today is to magically *create* the truth through indeterminacy and nominalism. According to this view, the truth is not an expression of what is; the truth is created by teaching people that believing is seeing – which is true in reverse. The role of the media is to convince people that the truth is what the elites of society want it to be. For the media pragmatists, truth is not what is, but what they say it is. "I make the news" is the common phrase in the press today.

The question for this book, then, is what does this pragmatist assault on your consciousness, your reality, do to you if you are incapable of questioning their reverse thinking? When you ask the question, "What should I do?" their answer is the following:

You should trust your feelings and give in to the will of the majority. We only tell you the truth and our main concern is the welfare of society. You should care about what others think and need. Your goal in life should be to alleviate suffering and make life better for others. So, you must sacrifice your earnings to the Afghanis and the immigrants on our southern border – and you should vote for the (lying) President we support.

Altruism, human sacrifice, is the one idea that both left and right support – yet it is the one idea that has caused millions to die through genocidal murder. It is the one idea that will keep the leftists in power as they kill and plunder society without mercy. It is the one idea that energizes dictatorships when they declare that "these people will not go along with the agenda of sacrifice; they insist on living their own lives and thinking for themselves; therefore, they must die." I have asked the question: "Quo Vadis?" Where are you marching?

What is wrong with the idea of invoking altruism as the solution to every problem and why do moral authorities think that doing so is the practical (pragmatic) thing to recommend? Why are they so convinced that invoking guilt in you is the right thing to do? Do you feel the soft cry of moral bullying involved here? Do you wonder about your future and who will take care of you when you have run out of money? What about that tinge of guilt you feel about wanting a better life? Answer these questions.

Finally, what does the "will of the majority" have to do with what you are supposed to think? What makes the will of the majority true by any means? Only pragmatism could claim this. Why shouldn't individuals with their own minds look toward the facts of existence before deciding what they should do? You must answer this question too before you turn society over to the destroyers; before you vote for your own destruction.

One of the key elements of critical theory is the development of anti-concepts that deceive people about important ideas.

"An anti-concept is an unnecessary and rationally unusable term designed to replace and obliterate some legitimate concept. The use of anti-concepts gives the listeners a sense of approximate understanding. But in the realm of cognition, nothing is as bad as the approximate . . . ."[11]

When we say that an anti-concept is unnecessary, we mean that it is not cognitively useful. We don't need it to help us understand reality and, as anti-concepts go, it leads to cognitive failure which is the inability to understand reality or gain true knowledge.

Let us examine one of today's anti-concepts. Let us use the concept of "critical race theory". How is it unnecessary and how is it rationally unusable?

Critical race theory is an aspect of the idea of critical theory in general. It involves the use of collective anti-concepts and the attribution of a thought pattern to individuals identified as members of a particular group. Critical race theory is derived from the same sources as the Aryan-based blood racism,

---

[11] Ayn Rand Lexicon

tribalism, collectivism, and human sacrifice. I wrote about it in my booklet, A Primer Against Racism:

"The fathers of modern racism (what I call racial theory), the men who brought such ideas into the twentieth century, were Arthur de Gobineau (Frenchman, b. July 14, 1816, d. Oct. 13, 1882) and Houston Steward Chamberlain (Anglo-German b. Sept. 9, 1855, d. Jan. 9, 1927). They believed that Nordic or Aryan men were a superior "race" destined to dominate history. They postulated that other "races" were inferior, and they warned that if the Aryan race did not preserve its racial purity, it would decline and become inferior as well. Through convoluted analyses that can best be described as pseudo-science, they purported to prove that specific characteristics were genetically (through the blood) linked to certain groups.

"20th Century racism is practiced by some who consider themselves members of this Aryan "race" and by their victims in reverse. Although there have been racial elements in the views of many nations and groups, this Aryan-based view is the major trend during the last two hundred or so years. (This is not to say that many "white" people are the most racist today. Many of them are sincere about eliminating the racism in our society, though many do not know how to do it, and they quietly question the open racism of others.)

"Although it is possible to divide human beings according to skin color or the geographic origin of their ancestors, there is nothing to be gained from it on a fundamental level. The method of dividing an idea into smaller units should allow us to better understand it in the process. If it does not, then the division is useless and cognitively dangerous. Race divisions do not help us understand "man." Nor do they help us understand the individuals who are classified into races. In fact, they are the sources of confusion and misunderstanding. The term "race," as used by Chamberlain and Gobineau, established an artificial idea. The correct term, scientifically, should have been "species." Nevertheless, because racial theory was regarded as "scientific," the term "race" soon replaced "species" in the minds of many and allowed for the assignment of negative characteristics to arbitrarily defined groups.

"In fact, the term "race" was used throughout much of recorded history to identify different tribes or ethnic groups. It was seldom used to designate a fundamental division of human beings as it is used in racial theory. The word was transformed by racial theory into a "scientific" designation, signifying distinct and fundamental differences among human beings using non-fundamental characteristics as distinguishing criteria. In effect, the term "race" has been stolen from history with its meaning twisted without scientific foundation. The continent of Europe was duped by racial theory, not without some willingness, into transforming the term "race" from its original non-fundamental meaning into a fundamental division of human beings.

"Scientifically speaking there is no such thing as a "race." The Human Being is one species of animal. The characteristics that differentiate certain groups of people do not determine intelligence or moral "capacity." They are characteristics that have enabled the survival of those living in a particular climate over a period. The principle of adaptation has allowed survival in each case. Survivors prevailed because they harbored genetic qualities that allowed them to continue. Their descendants today have inherited their genetic qualities.

"By the criteria used to define a biologically distinct species, the human being cannot be divided. The different colored men on earth have not been apart long enough, in biologic time scales, to eliminate their ability to interbreed. Their superficial differences are not fundamental divisions and mean nothing. Recorded history shows that human beings from many parts of the world have had almost constant contact and therefore could not have separated into different species. This sort of "mixing" must have taken place throughout many of the four million years that man is thought to have walked the earth. Therefore, all human beings alive today are members of one species: "man."

"Skin color does not make us different in a fundamental sense. It is a result of natural selection over centuries and reflects only the geographic area where our recent ancestors lived, the climates they frequented. It connotes no characteristic that defines character or the right to be a member of humanity. It is not a fundamental dividing line.

"Nor does skin color make a group uncivilized. The level of civilization a group has attained has to do with the level of intellectual development attained and the institutions created to deal with important matters. Higher levels of civilization were reached by groups living in virtually every part of the world and with every division of physical characteristics. There is no basis for Gobineau's idea that certain colored men cannot reach high civilization. The Egyptians (whose history includes African blacks), the Greeks, the Chinese, the Mesoamerican are only a few of the people who have developed great civilizations. Except for the Greeks, none of these groups was Aryan. The list of contributions to man's well-being from each constitutes the best that modern man has available. All of these civilizations contributed much to the areas of social organization, military advances, agricultural advances, architectural advances, mathematics, and the natural sciences. Nothing points to their inferiority.

"The same is true of any of the other characteristics that have been used to divide human beings into races. These characteristics are superficial elements, those most likely to be different from individual to individual. None have anything to do with the fundamental characteristics that define "man."

"Characteristics like "rational consciousness" and "conceptual capacity," which even though qualitatively different from person to person, are not so different that we can divide men into meaningful and separate species because of them. The capacities of rationality and conceptuality are what make man what he is, and as such are characteristic of every person regardless of any other characteristics. Since the use of the rational capacity must be consciously chosen, characteristics that reveal character and moral worth are derivative of this choice, not of any genetic or "racial" predisposition.

"What makes human beings different from one another is the extent to which they are rational.

Certainly, there are environmental influences, the metaphysical and epistemological premises that come from the culture, sub-culture, neighborhood, or parents that do much to sway a person. But it is the level of a person's thinking, the quality of his thinking that determines largely who he becomes and whether he or she succeeds.

"On the other side of this issue, many of the ideas (collectivism, dictatorship, and racism, to name a few) that have contributed to destruction and decline are considered by some, to be characteristic of the Aryan culture every bit as much as they are of those cultures they considered inferior. Yet, the Aryan according to racial theory is considered genetically superior. On this issue, it proves only that many Aryans could be just as "primitive" as many of those they called "savages." Genetics does not determine whether people will choose to think logically.

"Throughout the period of the development of European racial theory, what is singularly lacking is an effort to define which characteristics make up a distinct race. This question has been avoided (with a few failed exceptions) because it cannot be answered. Do we use skin color, geographic origin, cranial size, brain size, body or facial structure, hair color, eye color, intelligence, height, nose, chin or any of a number of other characteristics? Which of these (or which of these in combination) can help us define a race? The answer is none because none is fundamental, none clearly defines the humanity in us and none can be supported by valid argument.

"Why do we even need to ask the question? What does it mean in a fundamental sense? Why is it relevant, and why do we need to develop social policy, particularly political discrimination and exclusion, around such superficial characteristics? If racial policy is based on these kinds of superficial characteristics, then that makes "race" an inapplicable idea, unnecessary and cognitively dangerous. Race divisions are then one of the most fundamental, focal and devastating mistakes of man's history.

"During the 19th Century, the ideas of Gobineau had won out in Germany and much of Europe. He influenced such major figures as Richard Wagner, Friedrich Nietzsche, and Adolf Hitler not to mention the entire philosophical development of Europe. Because the German and French intellectuals who agreed with him were the most important in Europe, their racist premises clouded the views of even some of the most honest intellectuals of the time. Racial theory was virtually "absorbed" into the fundamental premises of the European philosophical foundation (and later our philosophical foundation). The few honest intellectuals of the time, lacking the advantage of hindsight, did not realize what would be done in the name of Aryan superiority, and how devastating would be the impact of such ideas on the people who would live out the tragedies that would ensue. Their effect was to transform the earlier European ideas of imperialism, domination and conquest (and all the bloodshed that such ideas entailed) and bring them into the 20th Century. Their effect was not only to release Hitler on the world, but to set into the psyche of the European, and many influenced by him, the idea that to be European and Aryan meant that one was master of reality, the owner of the right to dominate all nations, the standard by which one judged intelligence, beauty, and superiority. That such an idea is implicit in the views and actions of many today has barely been noticed. What is more important, we have overlooked that these ideas have influenced all men and women of all colors and national origins who were educated in America; that means even the victims of racism, discrimination, and prejudice. Even those who would like to destroy the influence of European philosophy (leftists, progressives, communists, socialists, multiculturalists) are using the very European ideas that are part of racial theory, the collectivism, the categorizing of groups into races, the assignment of superior versus inferior markers, etc. While they insist that Western philosophy is corrupt, they are practicing it and its most deadly elements: separation, hatred, demonization, vilification, and domination.

"The very idea, then, that races exist is racism. This is the problem at its root. Those who claim they are trying to fight racism are racist when they talk as if "races" were valid divisions of man. Whether it is done innocently or not (and it is often done without malice), thinking that races exist keeps people thinking racially.

"Such thinking is found in the collectivist catch-phrases of the day, in the politically correct language with which we are being inundated. If you believe that there are racial collectives and you base your discussions with others on such a foundation, you are racist. Am I changing the definition of racism? No. This is the true definition based upon the fact that race is an improper division of human beings. It is, therefore, the definition that our culture has evaded.

"Each of us needs to recognize that, to the extent that we do not question the existence of races, we are still dependent on racism's cultural and philosophical heritage. It is not a heritage that we living today created (white or black). Few of us are philosophers, capable of discerning the contradictions in our inherited history and ideas. We are dependent upon our philosophers and intellectuals for this, and they have not done their work well. They too have accepted collectivist and racist traditions and have not questioned them adequately. That is why we find ourselves in this situation today."[12]

So, when the left creates a "racial theory" utilizing the same basic arguments as the original racial theory of the Anglo scholars, they are essentially creating a different superior race, this time the superior race is any race that is not white – and the inferior race, because his subconscious thoughts (not his blood) make up his evil character, is every white man, although one cannot read minds. Just like blood was a false racial argument, now skin color is the new false racial argument.

This makes critical race theory into a cognitive nightmare. One cannot "see" or understand a race according to this racial idea because it is not intended to create cognitive clarity. In fact, it is impossible to define a race; such a concept is nonexistent. It does not exist and there is no scientific foundation for it. Although there are

---

[12] Individualism by Robert Villegas https://amzn.to/3vUtzr9 (paid link)

people of various shades of color, there is no such thing as a white person with specific characterological aspects. There is no such thing as a white person except people without melanin in their skin (albinos) and these people have a particular skin abnormality. They are not evil by nature.

Additionally, one cannot identify the race of a person by looking at genetic traits. There is no specific gene for the race of a person. This means that the identification of specific races and their "endemic" characteristics is anti-conceptual, fruitless. When we bring "race" into a discussion, we are bringing cognitive inefficacy into it, and this explains why "race" issues are so difficult to understand and communicate effectively. As I have said before, there is no such thing as a race so critical race theory is a false concept; inefficacious and based upon ignorance.

Another consequence of any racial theory is the false designation of collectives that divide people. The Nazis were able to separate out of their society people from numerous nations, making quasi-valid races out of those people because of their various skin colors. Therefore, they jailed Jews, Spaniards, and other nationalities – those people were not German. Today, the divisions are much the same; people of darker skin colors and semi-primitive cultures are thought to be superior specifically because their skin and/or culture is not built on the back of the so-called European "white" culture. So, if your "group" is not European, then you should be given favorable treatment above the treatment accorded "whites".

If "white" culture is supposed to have predatory qualities or if someone with darker skin chooses the "white" ideas of the Enlightenment, does that mean they subconsciously advocate slavery, conquest, even logic and intelligent thinking? Does that make the person of darker color "white"? I say, conceptually, they can't do that and prosper. This contradiction exposes the flaw in holding skin color to be indicative of anything. The anti-concept of a race does not exist in any fundamental sense.

Imagine then, you were raised to be color blind. Imagine you did not think you were superior to anyone. Imagine, also, throughout your entire life, you have striven to be fair to every individual you have met. If your skin is "white", as the term is generally thought, how could you be a racist? This exposes the lie about what races are and the truth of the fact that you cannot make viable public policy through anti-concepts that are defined by means of pseudo-science. Any person who thinks this way can only cry the soft cry of race divisions. The only solution is to treat every person as an individual, to judge him or her according to the qualities of character they have chosen and refuse to think of collective divisions of men. Only individuals exist – races do not.

Keep in mind that many white people died to liberate slaves during the Civil War. Additionally, many corporations have opened their hiring doors to people regardless of skin color and have shown exemplary behavior when it comes to treating all their employees fairly and rewarding them well for their hard work. None of this is supposed to matter. How is a so-called "color-blind" person supposed to feel when he is told that he is automatically racist because his skin is "white"? This must be a huge soft cry for people who are told to apologize for being white and declared persona non grata.

The Soft Cry of Modern Philosophy

Something happened to the mind with the advent of Descartes, Hume, and Kant (among others). The mind influenced by these "esteemed" men was sent into a swamp of indeterminacy and smacked by the spoon (philosophy) that fed him. Starting with the Platonic realms, they deduced that reality had two realms, one of nonexistence and the other of indeterminacy. This left man an orphan without intellectual guidance. The individual, taught by the students of modern philosophy, was left in a desert without an oasis.

As we study the major psychological theorists, we can't help being struct by the number of terms they invent to identify specific principles of psychology, as well as the principles of metaphysics and epistemology. Just like every philosopher, every psychologist must entrap you in his or her terminology to guide your mind. I view these "buzzword trap" gambits as excessive and unhelpful. They are central to the corruption of the psychological and philosophical mind of man. They represent the framework of the soft cry of the modern mind.

Aristotle and (somewhat) Plato, making their works obsolete and uninteresting. Major concepts were also swept away and forgotten by the average mind

– and then they were stolen and redefined by modern philosophers to provide substance for the fanciful notions of Kant, Hume, Dewey, and others. This gave way to anti-concepts and arbitrary explosions of mystical nonsense (ESP, transcendence, magic, miracles, mystification of history, neurosis, paranoia, and schizophrenia to name a few) that bred anti-values and, eventually, nihilism. The soft cry of the mind was the result.

Yet, one important investigation (that has barely been done) is how the falsehoods and arbitrariness of modern philosophy have affected the mind of man and created his psychology (his soft cry). It starts, not with psychology, but with epistemology and how man defines his concepts.

The first most important issues an individual confronts in life is who he is and how he can learn about it. For this, he requires clear thinking about several important issues, but this is not something he can deal with at a young age. Yet, almost every child is confronted with "adult" issues such as who he is, what should he do and from where does he come. More than this, unless he is a favored child, he will be confronted by the injunction to sacrifice for others. This comes from modern philosophy too, yet the child is under five years old.

When he goes to university, he is taught the precepts of modern philosophy. The straight jacket begins to engulf him. I wrote about this in my book, "What Harvard and Princeton Don't want You to know". I would suggest you read this book if you want to learn more on the critical matter of how our minds today are being destroyed by the professors who taught the professors who taught the professors about pragmatism and its deadly consequences.

The soft cry begins when the individual is berated by someone older about his behavior. He would not have engaged in what is called bad behavior had he known there was something "wrong" about what he had done. I remember my first berating at about my first year of school – which was a progressive kindergarten. My teacher had berated me for being selfish about a toy that another kid had tried to take away from me. She told my mother about this cruelty of mine and suggested that I be made to learn the lesson of altruism which she called "love for others".

The teacher did not explain the foundations of altruism which were the metaphysical and epistemological principles of Descartes, Hume, Kant, and Dewey. The source of altruism for her were the buzzwords of sacrifice which have been converted by modern philosophy into the political buzzword we know today as re-distribution.

She did not tell me about Hume and Kant. She likely did not know about them. She likely did not know about Dewey, or that his ideas likely came from the materials which taught her how to be a kindergarten teacher. Everything she was taught was likely integrated by her as a set of precepts which made her into a good teacher. She probably thought she was being a good teacher whenever she punished selfishness and every other kid who did not like to be forced to comply with thieving child.

She thought she was a good teacher to encourage "getting along" for the students. She thought she was a good teacher to act as a "policeman" against selfishness by any student. She thought she was a good teacher to encourage each student to think, above all, about how to appease the mob. She was probably very proud of how she did her job and felt wonderful that she was teaching children how to be "good" citizens and dutiful slaves. If you don't think this teacher was creating the "soft cry" of modern philosophy, without knowing it, then you don't know what Harvard and Princeton don't want you to know.

The Solution

As a person grapples with his innocence and mistakes, the constant attacks on him make it difficult to live a moral life. In fact, there is a singular missing concept that, if accepted and practiced, would wipe away life-long misery. This is the concept that should replace all doubt and guilt. It is called egoism.

An egoist not a narcissist, as is commonly thought. The true egoist is free of guilt; he has no incentive to act out revenge or cruelty towards others. An egoist is not required to declare universal love toward all men, but, after himself, all others are equal – not better. Because he or she is not prejudiced towards others (which means pre-judgment of others based upon a collective standard), he or she tends to give others the benefit of the doubt.

In fact, most children are born naturally egoistic. They come with a sense of natural self-worth and open-eyed wonder about the world. It is only when they are asked to turn into shmoos who think only about others first; when they are asked to give to others and conform to the Deweyan commandment to think what others think first, that they become mini progressives seeking to make everyone around them smile at them for their "giving" natures and willingness to join the group. It is then when they become neurotic, self-deprecating, and paranoid. It is then when they feel uncomfortable as they wonder if they are doing enough "good" to make the world love them.

Any individual who has spent his years sleeplessly wondering about what is wrong with him; who has experienced the nightmares that tell him he is wilfully evil, wilfully wrong, guilty, and sinful; who has experienced a massive doubt created by anti-egoism, can be stripped clean if he or she realizes that he has a right to be self-driven, forward driven and innocent. It is the fortunate individual who refuses to bend to the wills of others. It is this person who seldom experiences the soft cry created by modern philosophy, modern psychology, and modern education.

Indeed, modern psychology teaches him that his problem is that he loves sex, modern philosophy teaches him his problem is that he loves himself while Dewey teaches his teachers that his problem is that he doesn't love others first. Don't be surprised that later he will join a criminal gang and steal on the streets – all for the sake of his collective. After all, he has been taught in school to put the gang first, that pride comes from defending his pals against the biggest gang which is society. Don't be surprised that he will hate capitalism (freedom) and live like a

Sicilian drug lord killing others for the honor of being a "made man", of being loved by his group. It is all in the education. You never knew that Kant and Dewey were the ultimate criminal masterminds, did you?

Once the individual realizes, after many years, that he or she has a right to an objective appraisal of his or her ego, based upon objective knowledge and objective morality, he or she will eventually grow a love of the ego. To accomplish this, the individual must reject the subjectivism that comes with mysticism, rationalism, and altruistic self-sacrifice.

This is the moment when the individual eliminates the fears beneath his soft cry and accepts reason, not emotions, as the solution for life. At this moment, the individual learns not to fear altruism, government, collectivism, media lies, and the dreaded modern philosophy and all the lies that float around him. Once he or she realizes that thinking has been made chaotic by the constant stream of indoctrination and moral imperatives (that have nothing to do with his or her wellbeing and everything to do with the destruction of concepts, knowledge, and values). In fact, as the individual pursues truth, he realizes that the force that causes all the lies and even the soft cry of guilt of the individual is modern philosophy, the ideas of indeterminacy, irrationalism, and cosmic chaos (nihilism).

When he or she begins to understand the role and the purpose of ideas such as the individual, the mind, knowledge, moral action, and individualism, he or she comes to recognize that they are all contained in the concept of the ego and its role in the world. It is then when he or she recognizes individual rights, property rights, and individual autonomy. During this process, he or she and arrives at a point when collectivism, altruism and love of others is diametrically opposed to his self and his mind.

There is a limit to the amount of nonsense your mind can absorb. At some point, you must resist the irrational, and you must have the courage to challenge the false concepts imposed upon you by religion and modern philosophy. You must dive into the abyss of the soft cry and make your new understanding explicit. You must challenge the unfairness of altruism and realize that you owe love only to yourself and to those who love you without exploiting you.

The haters, the practitioners of modern philosophy (especially pragmatism) will threaten you with jail or burning in Hell. But the truth is, there is no punishment worse than the punishment of accepting lies, their gaslighting, their pseudo-science and their idea laundering. It is these tools they have used to turn you into their slave who must work for them, live for them, and die for them. Once you throw off these demands, once you accept the sanctity of your ego and the worthiness of your mind, you can start living.

There is a major reason why most people are not aware of the importance of their egos and why it is important that they have a high level of self-love. This is because of the overwhelming power of the educational system that preaches the idea that man should not trust or love his self. Most people never resist this powerful indoctrination in our social institutions, and they allow teachers to shame them and scare them out of living. If the individual even minutely thinks that his self is important to him, he will be made to feel guilty for having pride and self-love. He will have to accept their intellectual straight jacket or else.

Whenever you try to give self-love, you are confronted consciously and subconsciously with the overwhelming gargantuan of "they" who know that you are wrong for feeling self-regard. You feel overwhelmed by a sense of guilt, and this creates internal tension and depression. You learn to repress your love of self and you hope the idea goes away and never returns. You descend into a life of giving and never taking. You feel bad about your self, and decide that the only way to feel good is to go along with the orgy of giving to others and hating your self.

This soft cry of self-hate is the state of mind too many people live under for far too many years. They do not know that their only salvation is to discover the power of the ego to make life better. They do not know that fighting self-love is the scourge of the subjective evil that haunts life. They do not know that the admonitions they receive from teachers and peers can only be met by declaring "I am morally right. I am innocent and I have done nothing wrong." With this victory, the soft cry of moral doubt transforms into the conviction that you possess true value and that the "others" are the bringers of hate.

In fact, many people praise the altruist because he or she supposedly cares for others. They see this trait as positive and point out the many things that altruists are supposed to do for others. I submit that it is the egoist who has the best attitude toward others because he or she recognizes his own values and chooses to value through morally chosen action. It is the egoist who sees all individuals as worthy of respect and equal treatment.

Unearned guilt makes you dislike yourself (gives you the soft cry). On the other hand, the more you experience your ego without guilt, the more you like yourself. This is an important point specifically because it points out the importance of asserting your ego and liking yourself as much as possible. This is where positive affirmations, contemplated and expressed often, to yourself, privately and even among others, can help you become a stronger, freer, and more successful individual.[13]

---

[13] Parenthetically, you can find some excellent exercises in my other books about positive affirmations and using the principle of positivity in two of my books. The first is "The REAL Purpose-Driven Life" at https://amzn.to/37vOFRM, and the companion book "Values and Purpose Workbook" https://amzn.to/3pHShXr. You will also find these exercises in my books "Rational Meditation" https://amzn.to/3pHSREB and the upcoming companion book yet to be published. All links are paid links.

SPEAKING FREELY

I am an American writer born in Weslaco, TX. I consider myself to be an independent philosopher with a strong influence from Objectivism, the philosophy of Ayn Rand. I have been studying and applying Objectivism to my writing and professional career since an early age.

I spent over twenty-seven years as a UPS executive in Indiana and worked in locations all over Europe such as Germany, England, and Spain. At UPS I worked in various positions including Sales Manager, Call Center Manager and Telecommunications Manager. I was involved in helping to transition UPS from paper-based processes to computerized networks and digital record keeping. I worked with early digital technologies and was one of the first telecommunications managers to use technology for communicating to drivers while they were on their routes. My system caught the attention of our national group and influenced the development of the computerized clipboard at UPS. Other developments I made also had impacts on national UPS programs including account management, Gantt charting, complaint processing, and the development of outbound teleservices and sales departments.

My Business Philosophy developed through fifty plus years of experience in several fields including transportation and technology (UPS), telecommunications (PACER and UPS), call center management (UPS), sales management (UPS and others), Internet (Nextera and other companies), network design and implementation (UPS), technical and marketing writing (PACER and Nextera) and motorsport marketing (SponsorProAZ, Insight Marketing Group and several teams and drivers).

I studied free market economics through the writings of Mises, Hayek, Rand, Hazlitt, Friedman, and others and attended lectures by prominent economists. I also read voraciously and attended lectures about philosophy and the history of philosophy, business philosophy, sales history and methodology and worked as a marketing and technical writer, website designer and telecommunications manager as well as call center manager. During those years, I created presentations for high level investor meetings in NYC, Miami, San Francisco, Minneapolis, and many other locations. I designed trade show displays and traveled extensively designing and installing computer network software and call center networks in Munich, Frankfort, Dusseldorf, London, Singapore, and Madrid. I have written over 260 business plans, mostly for start-ups in Canada and the USA. I learned not only how to work for top level CEOs and VPs but also how to help them be successful.

Over the years, I was fortunate to have met many influential people, saw several of the royals in London and worked for well-known athletes, racing drivers and entertainment professionals and celebrities.

After leaving UPS, I started my own sport marketing company specializing in writing sponsorship proposals for race car drivers and other athletes. Clients included Johnny Parsons, Jeff Ward, Larry Foyt, Ike Runnels, Jimmy Ward, Pat Golden, Steve Newey and Alexander Rossi to name a few. I also created many successful sales presentations and marketing documents for companies in New York City, San Francisco, Boston, San Francisco, Sacramento, Chicago, Miami, Minneapolis, Vancouver BC, and other locations.

Since 2015, I have written about 95 books in areas such as novels, theater, religion, poetry, philosophy, and business with a strong emphasis on philosophy and philosophical analysis. I have also written successful grant proposals for several organizations, earning millions of dollars for fire departments and charitable organizations.

I was mostly educated in Indiana and earned a Degree through the University of the State of NY (Albany) via an external degree program (when I came out of the military). I also served in the US Military as a communications specialist serving a tour of duty in Korea (during the Vietnam era) near the DMZ. I presently live in Arizona.

These four books by Robert Villegas comprise some of the business books that he has written. As an executive working for several companies, he was able to develop these methods that will help anyone seeking to excel in the business world. These books are:

How to Be a Great Employee – and a Greater Manager

You cannot be a great manager without first being a great employee. And this is something that requires learning, experience and attitude. The attitude comes from you but the learning and experience you should acquire through diligent study and practice. http://amzn.to/2BqdG2i $3.99 Kindle $8.95 softcover

SWOT Analysis Supercharged

A SWOT Analysis is an objective look at the internal and external elements of your organization that impact your success or lack thereof. If done diligently, you will always have a handle on what you need to do to improve season after season. http://amzn.to/2BCAWYx $3.99 Kindle $6.95 softcover

The Five-Module Call Center Training System

The Five-Module Call Center Training System is designed to assist the Call Center Team Leader in helping his employees quickly upgrade their skills to an acceptable level. http://amzn.to/2B3Svj1 $3.99 Kindle $5.95 softcover

Website Development Methodology

Effective strategic marketing requires the ability to differentiate the website development organization and its deliverables from those of the competition. http://amzn.to/2DnYMqh $2.99 Kindle $12.95 softcover.

www.robertvillegas.com

These four books comprise a system that can be used by both patients and counselors who are battling Alcoholism and Addiction. Based upon Mr. Villegas's own system developed during his struggle against alcoholism, this system includes:

Alcoholism and Addiction – A Secular Ten-Step Program

This groundbreaking book offers a secular approach to alcoholism unlike that offered by Alcoholics Anonymous. We recommend that every individual going for alcohol and drug-abuse counseling be given a copy of this book which contains the workbook and the two versions of The World's first drunk. http://amzn.to/2md6R9w $3.45 Kindle $11.95 softcover

The Secular Ten-Step Program Workbook

This booklet covers the program developed by Mr. Villegas. It is designed as a workbook with blank spaces for the patient to write his own thoughts as he takes each of the ten steps. Order one copy for each patient in counseling. http://amzn.to/2IrHimS $4.49 Kindle $6.95 softcover

The World's First Drunk – With Counselor Talking Points

This booklet is designed for the counselor as he works with patients during individual or group therapy. It contains helpful tips on discussing the life story of the man who invented alcohol. Order one copy for each patient in counseling. http://amzn.to/2I446Wr $2.99 Kindle $5.95 softcover

The World's First Drunk – Patient Version

This version of the short story contains empty spaces where the patient can answer questions about the life story of the man who invented alcohol. Order one copy for each counselor. http://amzn.to/2IdxBGb $2.99 Kindle $5.95 softcover.

www.robertvillegas.com

The Mark of Titus

Excerpts from the book Unkilling Jesus which highlight some of the key discoveries implied by new theories about the origin of the Jesus Myth. The idea that the Romans invented Christianity is the basic premise of new theories about the origin of Christianity.http://amzn.to/2itMCoO $3.49 Kindle $5.95 softcover

Contra Religion

This book is designed as a "shorter" explanation of the ideas presented in my larger book, "Behind the Ritual Mask" which seeks to define fundamental principles of religion. I'm hoping this book will serve as a primer for the original book and spur an interest in reading it. http://amzn.to/2yWMSlx $3.99 Kindle $6.95 softcover

Is this the Face that Launched a Thousand Ships?

It was love at first sight. I saw her one day while watching a television program about King Tut, whose tomb had been discovered by Howard Carter years before. I was looking at the famous bust of a beautiful Egyptian Queen. https://amzn.to/3t487x3 $3.99 Kindle $7.95 softcover

The History of Altruism

The History of Altruism is a historical treatment of the development of altruism throughout time from the Paleolithic period to today. It tracks the development of self-sacrifice of primitive man to the advent of altruism as a development from Kant's "duty". It covers a broad sweep of concepts and shows how they influenced modern man, religion and societies through the ages. https://amzn.to/3gN8zgy $4.19 Kindle 14.95 paperback.

www.robertvillegas.com

Unkilling Jesus

Who was Paul and what was his role in the creation of Christianity? What was his provenance, and did he meet the resurrected Christ? Who wrote Revelation and what was the document's purpose? Why was Domitian assassinated? http://amzn.to/2itMCo0 $3.99 Kindle $15.95 softcover

Domitian: The Final Messiah

The central goal of this book is to define the specific themes and concepts that make up Domitian's contribution to Christianity – in a sense, we are defining the specific Domitian overlay to the Christian materials originally developed for Titus. http://amzn.to/2yWMSlx $2.99 Kindle $6.95 softcover

Paul's Agon and the Mystification of History

Paul and Jesus are joined in one important way; the way of a miracle. They met on the road to Damascus while Paul supposedly pursued Christians. Jesus, in a sense, told Paul to get with the program and stop persecuting his people. In this incident, the Bible tells us that Jesus is already dead, and resurrected. This book argues otherwise. http://amzn.to/2zSDsuP $5.99 Kindle $19.95 softcover

Christianity on the Arch of Titus

This book explores the "persons" visible on the Triumphant Arch of Titus which is located in the heart of Rome. These people were significant in that they played a role, not only in Rome's conquest of Judaea but also in the creation of Christianity. This book explores those individuals and the roles they played in the creation of one of the most important religious movements in world history. https://amzn.to/3xz3OgM $3.69 Kindle 10.95 paperback.

www.robertvillegas.com

The REAL Purpose-Driven Life
After centuries of being told that it is not about you, it is time to set the record straight. You are a unique individual and your goal in life should be to achieve your own happiness.
https://amzn.to/2XyrpPf $3.50 Kindle $7.95 softcover

Values and Purpose Workbook
This book is about you. It's about time. After centuries of being told that nothing is about you, it is time to set the record straight. You are a unique individual and your goal in life should be to achieve your happiness. https://amzn.to/2XwlkTv $3.99 Kindle $8.95 softcover

www.robertvillegas.com

Poetic Prose and Poetry

These expressions represent some of Mr. Villegas' deepest thoughts as he lived and traveled throughout the world in locations such as Germany (East and West), Austria, Britain, Spain, Canada, France, Luxembourg, Belgium, the Netherlands, Korea, New York, Miami, San Francisco and other locations. https://amzn.to/3vu7X3B $2.99 Kindle $6.95 softcover

The Lost Poems

These poems were discovered among Mr. Villegas's archives in 2016. Many of them have been read by only Mr. Villegas. Most of these poems were rejected as "not that good". After seeing them again, he has changed his mind. These poems expressive, fresh and spontaneously honest. https://amzn.to/3aPg5nB $3.99 Kindle $6.95 softcover

Adam Reborn – A Short Play

Adam Reborn is a play of symbols. Adam and Eve, as I have portrayed them, are young and heroic people learning to deal with a Paradise and God that are hostile to them. There is no chance of life for them. https://amzn.to/3u9Nr8b $2.99 Kindle $6.95 softcover

The Boy Who Stood Alone

Jonny Payne has just discovered Ayn Rand and his parents don't know what to do. They take him to a priest and a psychologist but his only question is "What is the price of independence? https://amzn.to/3nCG6ve $3.99 Kindle $6.95 paperback.

www.robertvillegas.com

Aphrodite

Johnny is a Spanish guitar player with a mysterious past. At a party, he meets the beautiful songstress Aphrodite who is enthralled with his flamenco guitar skills. Later, she learns they have a connection, a particular song they both appear to know. Aphrodite discovers the connection, and through dreams, the two fall in love. The question is whether they will ever be together. https://amzn.to/3xIlmXZ $3.99 Kindle $5.95 softcover

The Odyssey of Amerigo the Founder

Amerigo was born in a time of desperation and dystopia. He was the only man with the vision of a great future. Many repaired to his cause while others swore to destroy him. They wanted his life, his mind and everything he loved. He swore that no matter what they did, he would win the struggle for freedom and a new future. https://amzn.to/2Qz8h2t $3.99 Kindle $8.95 softcover

Bob and Bobbie

1967 - a town outside Camp Casey, Korea - two young people have come together to challenge a world that makes love impossible. https://amzn.to/3sZWSpf $2.99 Kindle $5.95 softcover

The Raven Haired Girl

Bobby met Angie 52 years ago in a poor neighborhood in Indianapolis. It was love at first sight. For a few short months, their relationship blossomed into love. They were in love but didn't know how to be in love because they were only fourteen years old. https://amzn.to/3306plF $2.99 Kindle $6.95 paperback.

www.robertvillegas.com

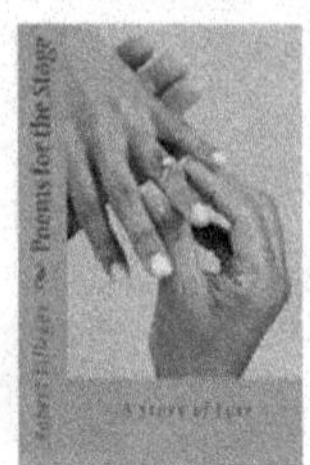 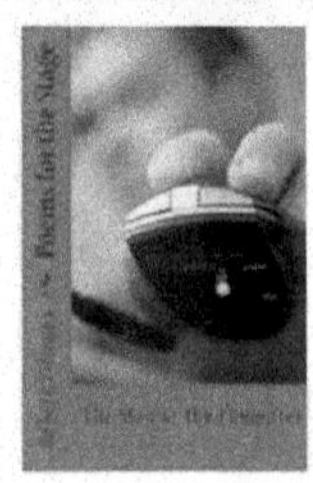

Poems for the Stage – A Story of Love

This dramatic presentation features poems found in Mr. Villegas's book Poetic Prose and Poetry. Some are also found in his book.

https://amzn.to/3gSJctV $2.99 Kindle $5.95 softcover

Poems for the Stage – The Man at the Computer

This dramatic presentation is based upon poems from Mr. Villegas's book Poetic Prose and Poetry. Some of the poems have been slightly altered to reflect the internal story. Mr. Villegas's book Poetic Prose and Poetry can be found on Amazon.com.

https://amzn.to/2R8zpFf $2.99 Kindle $5.95 softcover

www.robertvillegas.com

A Boomer takes on the Far Left

I just learned something about myself – and it isn't very good. In fact, it is very bad. I learned that the opinions of Boomers don't matter any more. We are obsolete in this new age of new knowledge. Anything we think is unimportant and false. I don't think so. https://amzn.to/3tzNqtc $5.19 Kindle $10.95 softcover

Crushing the Alinsky Radicals

The worst enemy of individual rights today is a group of people I call the Alinsky Radicals. These people are now in charge of our culture and temporarily, in charge of government. They are associated, philosophically and politically, with the communists and fascists of the past. They are not your father's liberals. They are the direct descendants of dictators such as Stalin and Mao. In this book, I hope to convince you of the evil of the Alinsky Radicals and to provide the intellectual ammunition you need to eradicate them from society. https://amzn.to/3hbh9WN $3.49 Kindle $8.95 softcover

The Conservative's Dilemma

I wrote this book to ask some important questions about the conservative philosophy of altruism. https://amzn.to/3bfDQ8e $2.99 Kinde $6.95 softcover.

The Biggest Mistakes in History – 2008 to 2016

To be the Chief Executive of the greatest country in the world requires a leader with a great deal of knowledge, experience and reasoning ability. It requires having the very best minds as advisors, minds that the President can count on to give reasoned arguments and detailed knowledge about the important issues of the day. I think it takes a special ability to understand the principle of cause and effect concerning how government action impacts the lives of real people. https://amzn.to/3tDQ4Ol $2.99 Kindle $10.95 softcover

www.robertvillegas.com

Dachau and Berlin in 1990

This booklet chronicles Mr. Villegas' thoughts during visits to Dachau and Berlin during 1990, disclosing my observations of milestones in German history, past and present, and relating those events to world happenings as they were unfolding at the time. I traveled throughout Germany for much of 1990 while on business. https://amzn.to/3ex578d $2.99 Kindle $6.95 softcover

What Harvard and Princeton Don't Want You to Know

The professors at Harvard and Princeton don't want you to know about the worst ideas in history. This is because they have been pawning these ideas off as true and profound. They have been using them to deceive and manipulate us for centuries. https://amzn.to/3farP5p $5.19 Kindle $9.95 softcover

Defending American Values

This book is made up of several chapters about American values and how they can be defended without a descent into the abyss of dictatorship. The book argues for individual rights and provides reasons why we should fight for them. https://amzn.to/3uMFq9L $3.99 Kinde $5.95 softcover.

Capitalism Doesn't Fail

How many times have we heard the old saw: "Capitalism has failed again" over the course of contemporary events? We heard it during the Great Depression of 1929 after Hoover had invoked tariffs and precipitated economic retaliation and a banking crisis. Along with this question usually came a statement to the effect, that "We can fix capitalism and make it even stronger by issuing economic controls or spending money to stimulate economic activity." This book will argue that capitalism, as an economic system, cannot fail as long as individuals are free to act. https://amzn.to/3xZIAJ6 $4.19 Kindle $10.95 softcover

www.robertvillegas.com

Finding Sponsors 1 and 2

This book is written for anyone seeking sponsorship relationships in the sport and entertainment fields. The ideas and principles presented here are applicable to any company, sport team, entertainment company, marketing agency and charitable organization that uses corporate sponsorships to support its activities. Volume 1: https://amzn.to/3ejm1Hp $5.19 Kindle $12.95 softcover Volume 2: https://amzn.to/3eVDoOe $4.69 Kindle $10.95 softcover

How to Write a Sponsorship Proposal

This booklet provide you with some basic guidelines on what to communicate in order to produce a winning sponsorship proposal. These guidelines will focus on what you should be presenting to your potential sponsor to make the best business case for involvement with your team or entertainment company. $2.99 Kindle $6.95 softcover

Hospitality Event Planning Handbook

One key part of your sponsorship activation strategy might be customer hospitality events in conjunction with sporting events. How do you pull off a Hospitality Event for your biggest customers? You may not know how to start, what to do and how to ensure the event is a success. This book can help. http://amzn.to/2mxzpgy $7.95 softcover.

Selling Sponsorship in the Age of the Coronavirus

This book provides suggestions on how sport teams, athletes and concert promoters can mitigate the damage done to their businesses by the economic lockdowns (due to the Coronavirus). It integrates checklists, SWOT Analysis and other valuable business aids into one toolkit that will help you keep your sport and/or genre alive in these difficult times. https://amzn.to/2QVBNiM $5.15 Kindle $5.95 softcover

www.robertvillegas.com

Finding Sponsors Forms Book

This "Forms Book" is intended to provide samples of the forms mentioned in my book "Finding Sponsors for Sport and Entertainment". This will make it possible for you to reproduce these forms in other formats as well as download the forms document from the SponsorProAZ website for use with Microsoft Word. https://amzn.to/3b95yDW $2.99 Kindle $5.50 softcover

Submitting Your Sponsorship Proposal Online

This booklet enables sport teams and concert promoters to submit their sponsorship proposals to companies that accept only online submission of proposals. https://amzn.to/3euzdti $2.99 Kindle $5.95 softcover

The Art of Sponsorship

This short book is based upon Mr. Villegas' book "Finding Sponsors for Sport and Entertainment". It is also based upon a course that he taught for an organization managing Indiana Parks and Recreation facilities. It is, in a sense, a condensation of information from the book geared toward organizations that would like to earn revenues on their facilities through corporate sponsorship. https://amzn.to/3beuVnC $2.99 Kinde $6.95 softcover.

Restarting Your Business After the Pandemic

This new book is designed to help you restart your business after the Coronavirus pandemic. You will find here all the right questions, how you can find the answers and the forms you need to walk through your restart and coming success. https://amzn.to/2QVBNiM $5.15 Kindle $5.95 softcover

www.robertvillegas.com